ANIMALS AT RISK

PRAIRIE DOGS IN DANGER

BY A. J. GRUCELLA

Gareth Stevens
Publishing

Please visit our website, www.garethstevens.com. For a free color catalog of all our high-quality books, call toll free 1-800-542-2595 or fax 1-877-542-2596.

Library of Congress Cataloging-in-Publication Data

Grucella, A.J.
Prairie Dogs in Danger / by A.J. Grucella.
 p. cm. — (Animals at risk)
Includes index.
ISBN 978-1-4339-9165-3 (pbk)
ISBN 978-1-4339-9166-0 (6-Pack)
ISBN 978-1-4339-9164-6 (library binding)
1. Prairie dogs — Juvenile literature. 2. Endangered species — Juvenile literature. I. Title.
QL737.R68 G78 2014
599.367—dc23

First Edition

Published in 2014 by
Gareth Stevens Publishing
111 East 14th Street, Suite 349
New York, NY 10003

Copyright © 2014 Gareth Stevens Publishing

Designer: Andrea Davison-Bartolotta
Editor: Therese M. Shea

Photo credits: Cover, pp. 1, 11, 13, 20 iStockphoto/Thinkstock; pp. 4, 14 Eric Isselee/Shutterstock.com; p. 5 Hemera/Thinkstock; p. 6 Karel Gallas/Shutterstock.com; p. 8 Dorling Kindersley RF/Thinkstock; p. 9 Danita Delimont/Gallo Images/Getty Images; p. 15 BerndtVorwald/Shutterstock.com; p. 17 Ethan Welty/Getty Images; p. 18 Vitoriano Junior/Shutterstock.com; p. 19 Doug Sokell/Visuals Unlimited/Getty Images; p. 21 Barbara Sax/AFP/Getty Images.

Printed in the United States of America

CPSIA compliance information: Batch #CS13GS: For further information contact Gareth Stevens, New York, New York at 1-800-542-2595.

CONTENTS

Words in the glossary appear in **bold** type the first time they are used in the text.

Definitely Not Dogs

What's small, lives underground, barks, and eats grass? A prairie dog! This little animal isn't a dog. It's a **rodent**. It's called a prairie dog because of where it lives and what it sounds like.

Prairie dogs live on the grasslands, or prairies, of North America, from Canada to Mexico. Settlers of the prairies called them dogs because they make a bark-like noise. They sometimes sound like a small dog yipping!

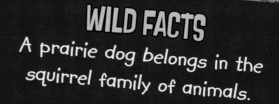

WILD FACTS
A prairie dog belongs in the squirrel family of animals.

 Prairie dogs are often seen standing on their back legs, looking out across the land.

LITTLE FURRY BODIES

Most prairie dogs are about 1 foot (30 cm) long. Their tail is another few inches. All prairie dogs have short legs and usually weigh no more than 4 pounds (1.8 kg). Their little bodies are covered with mostly brown or yellowish fur.

There are five **species** of prairie dogs: black-tailed, white-tailed, Mexican, Gunnison's, and Utah prairie dogs. The black-tailed prairie dog is the most common. The Mexican prairie dog is the rarest.

You can *see* in this photo how the black-tailed prairie dog got its name!

The Five Species of Prairie Dogs

SPECIES	LOCATION
white-tailed	Colorado, Utah, Wyoming, Montana
Gunnison's	New Mexico, Colorado, Arizona, Utah
Utah	Utah
black-tailed	Canada, western plains of United States, Mexico
Mexican	Mexico

Home Sweet Burrow

Prairie dogs may be small and furry, but they have long, sharp claws. They use these to dig underground **burrows**. The burrows have many tunnels and rooms. Just like your home, a prairie dog burrow has bedrooms—and even a bathroom!

Prairie dog burrows are marked on the surface by dirt mounds left behind after they dig. The mounds also let the little creatures stand a bit taller when they're looking out across the prairie for enemies.

DRAWING OF A PRAIRIE DOG BURROW

▼ The dirt mound at the entrance of a prairie dog burrow also keeps some bad weather from entering a prairie dog's home.

WILD FACTS
White-tailed, Gunnison's, and Utah prairie dogs **hibernate** in their burrows through winter.

PRAIRIE DOG TOWN

A family of prairie dogs is called a coterie (KOH-tuh-ree). It's usually made up of a male, one or more females, and their young. The coterie lives on about an acre (0.4 ha) of land. Each coterie **fiercely** guards this territory from other coteries.

Hundreds of black-tailed prairie dogs live together in a colony called a "town." Texas was home to the largest prairie dog town. Found in 1900, it was about 100 miles (160 km) wide and 250 miles (400 km) long.

WILD FACTS
The Texas prairie dog town may have had as many as 400 million prairie dogs!

11

DON'T MAKE THEM ANGRY!

If a prairie dog wanders into a coterie territory that isn't its own, there's trouble! First, the prairie dogs of the coterie try to scare the stranger away. They stare at it, chatter their teeth, bark, and even chase it until it leaves.

Coteries fight other prairie dogs over territory, but they work together against common enemies. Prairie dog predators include coyotes, snakes, hawks, and eagles. Prairie dogs take turns being lookouts for their neighborhood. If they see a predator, they warn their neighbors.

WILD FACTS
A prairie dog barks about 40 times per minute when it's warning others of danger!

Prairie dogs have different barks for different kinds of predators.

Not Just Noise?

After the predator has left, a prairie dog barks again to let everyone know it's safe to come out of the burrow. This bark sounds different than the warning. Prairie dogs have many different kinds of barks. People who study prairie dogs say they have a kind of language. They make sounds in a certain order and at a certain speed.

Besides sounds, prairie dogs **communicate** by smell and touch. They recognize each other by touching teeth!

Prairie dogs look like they're kissing when they touch teeth.

PROBLEMS ON THE PRAIRIE

Prairie dogs hunt for food during the day when it's easier to see predators. Besides grass, they eat other plants, roots, and seeds. In recent years, much of the prairie dog **habitat** has been taken over for farmland. Farmers often kill prairie dogs to save crops.

Ranchers kill prairie dogs so their livestock have grass to eat. Homes have been built over many prairie dog habitats as well. All these actions mean there are many fewer prairie dogs today. Some species are heading toward **extinction**.

WILD FACTS
An illness called sylvatic plague is another threat to prairie dogs. They get it from fleas.

It's legal to poison prairie dogs in some states.

POSSIBLE SOLUTIONS

Two prairie dog species are really in trouble. The Utah prairie dog is called "threatened," and the Mexican prairie dog is **endangered**. It's rarely seen anymore in Mexico.

Some organizations are working to help prairie dogs. One program moves the animals to places where they won't harm farmland. They keep prairie dogs in the special area by planting tall grass as a kind of fence. Prairie dogs don't like to travel through tall grass because they can't see what's beyond.

LOCATION OF MEXICAN PRAIRIE DOGS

 Even tough laws don't seem to be helping many prairie dog populations.

WHY WE NEED PRAIRIE DOGS

Why should we save prairie dogs? They do a lot for their habitat. Their burrows become homes for other animals such as rabbits, weasels, and foxes. They're also part of a food web, and many animals depend on them for food. Prairie dog digging is good for the soil as well.

What can you do about the prairie dog problem? Learn more about what's being done to help them! You can also write a letter or e-mail to government leaders telling them what you think.

Besides the many other reasons to save prairie dogs, they're cute!

GLOSSARY

burrow: a hole made by an animal in which it lives or hides

communicate: to share thoughts or feelings by sound or movement

endangered: in danger of dying out

extinction: the death of all members of a species

fiercely: in a manner that shows strong feelings

habitat: the natural place where an animal or plant lives

hibernate: to be in a sleeplike state for an extended period of time, usually during winter

rodent: a small, furry animal with large front teeth, such as a mouse or prairie dog

species: a group of plants or animals that are all of the same kind

For More Information

Books

Markle, Sandra. *Prairie Dogs.* Minneapolis, MN: Lerner Publications, 2007.

Rustad, Martha E. H. *Prairie Dogs and Their Burrows.* Mankato, MN: Capstone Press, 2005.

Websites

Mammals: Prairie Dog
www.sandiegozoo.org/animalbytes/t-prairie_dog.html
See many photos of prairie dogs on this zoo website.

Prairie Dog
animals.nationalgeographic.com/animals/mammals/prairie-dog/
See the map of the prairie dog habitat and hear what they sound like.

Prairie Dogs
www.defenders.org/prairie-dogs/prairie-dogs-101
Read more about prairie dogs as well as what you can do to help them.

INDEX

24

This book
belongs to
me

This 1995 edition published by Derrydale Books,
distributed by Random House Value Publishing, Inc.,
40 Engelhard Avenue, Avenel, New Jersey 07001.

Random House
New York • Toronto • London • Sydney • Auckland

A CIP catalog record for this book is available from the
Library of Congress

ISBN 0-517-12087-9

Brer Rabbit's Adventures

Illustrated
by
Rene Cloke

DERRYDALE BOOKS
NEW YORK • AVENEL

BRER RABBIT AND BRER FOX

Brer Rabbit was a naughty little fellow. He liked to play tricks on Brer Fox, Brer Wolf and the other animals who were always trying to catch him.

But Brer Rabbit was so clever that he managed to escape every time and went on playing his tricks.

One day, Brer Wolf and Brer Fox decided to put a stop to this so they made a plan.

"I've thought of a good idea," said Brer Wolf, "run home and get into bed and pretend to be dead and I will go to Brer Rabbit's house with the news. When Brer Rabbit comes to look at you, just jump up and catch him!"

"That should be easy," agreed Brer Fox and he trotted home and went to bed.

As soon as Brer Fox had gone, Brer Wolf went along to Brer Rabbit's house and called out—

"Are you there, Brer Rabbit? Sad news, poor Brer Fox died this morning. I'm just going around to tell his friends," and off he ran.

When the wolf had gone, Brer Rabbit sat down and thought hard. "This sounds like a trick," he said and decided to go to Brer Fox's house and see for himself if the fox was really dead.

When he got to Brer Fox's house, he walked carefully around to see if any traps were set and then he peeped into the window.

There was Brer Fox, lying on the bed, with his eyes shut so Brer Rabbit went to the open door.

"Poor Brer Fox," he said aloud, "I wonder if he is really dead? I think he must be for he lies very still; I had better wait here until his friends come."

Then he had another look at Brer Fox. "You can always tell when a fox is dead," he said, "because he keeps shaking his left leg."

When Brer Fox heard this, he thought he had better shake his leg but, of course, as soon as he did this, Brer Rabbit knew that he was just pretending.

He dashed out of the house and didn't stop running until he was safely home.

"They can't catch me with that trick," he laughed.

And he went on laughing all the time he was having his tea.

THE TAR-BABY

Brer Fox tried to think of a good way to catch Brer Rabbit but the rabbit was always too clever for him.

One day, Brer Fox worked out a new plan.

With a lot of tar he made a tar-baby, put a hat on its head and stuck it on a stick near Brer Rabbit's house; then he hid in some bushes and waited to see what would happen.

Before long, Brer Rabbit came walking by and, when he saw the tar-baby, he stopped and looked at it in surprise; he had never seen anything quite like that before.

"Good morning," said Brer Rabbit, "it's a fine day."

But the tar-baby didn't answer. "Can't you hear me?" shouted Brer Rabbit at the top of his voice.

But still the tar-baby didn't answer.

This made Brer Rabbit so angry that he rushed up and hit the tar-baby and, of course, his paw stuck to the tar.

"Let go," yelled Brer Rabbit, "or I'll hit you again!"

So he hit out with his other paws and those stuck as well.

There was Brer Rabbit stuck to the tar-baby and he couldn't get off.

Then Brer Fox walked out from the bushes and laughed, for this was just what he had hoped would happen.

"You seem to be stuck up this morning, Brer Rabbit," he said, "now I've caught you at last and I mean to punish you. You won't play any more tricks on me!"

Brer Rabbit thought quickly.

"Do what you like with me, Brer Fox," he cried, "but don't throw me into the briar patch!

Hang me or drown me but, *please*, don't throw me into the briar patch!"

"That must be the best way to hurt him," thought Brer Fox, so he pulled Brer Rabbit from the tar-baby and flung him into the briar patch.

"That will be the end of him!" he barked.

But, in a moment, Brer Rabbit had scrambled out.

"I was born and bred in a briar patch!" he laughed as he scampered home. "Born and bred in a briar patch!"

BRER RABBIT AND BRER TORTOISE

When Brer Rabbit was out one day, he saw Brer Fox hustling along with a sack over his shoulder; he seemed to be in a great hurry.

Something was kicking and shouting inside the sack.

"That sounds like someone I know," said Brer Rabbit, "I believe it's Brer Tortoise."

Now, Brer Tortoise was a friend of his, so the little rabbit decided that he must try and help him. He took a short cut through the forest to Brer Fox's house.

When he got there, he ran into the garden and tore up a lot of plants from the flower beds.

Then he hid by the front door.

After a time, Brer Fox appeared with the sack over his shoulder and Brer Rabbit called out—

"Fetch a big stick, Brer Fox! Someone is tearing up plants in your garden!"

Dropping the sack on the doorstep, Brer Fox took up a stick and rushed into the garden.

While he was searching for the rascal, Brer Rabbit undid the sack and let out his friend Brer Tortoise.

Then, between them, they took one of Brer Fox's beehives and stuffed it into the sack.

"That will give him a surprise!" whispered Brer Rabbit as they tied up the sack and put it back on the doorstep.

Brer Fox came back from the garden feeling very angry because he couldn't find anyone pulling up his plants. He picked up the sack and went into his house, slamming the door behind him.

Brer Rabbit and Brer Tortoise sat in the bushes and waited.

Then they heard a great noise of buzzing and yelping, and out ran Brer Fox with the angry bees buzzing around him and stinging him as he ran.

"I thought I had captured a tortoise in my sack!" howled Brer Fox. "How can I have made such a mistake?"

"Ha, ha!" laughed Brer Rabbit. "That will teach him to leave tortoises alone— they might turn into a hive of bees!"

The two friends hurried off before Brer Fox discovered that they had tricked him.

BRER RABBIT AND BRER FOX GO FISHING

On a very hot day, all the animals
were digging a patch of ground together
so that they could plant some vegetables.
As Brer Rabbit was rather small, he found it hard
work and after a time he threw down his fork and
called out—

"I've got a thorn in my paw, I must stop
and pull it out."

He walked off to a shady spot and
pretended to get the thorn from his paw.

Then he saw, a little way off, a well
with a bucket hanging from it.

"How cool that looks!" thought
Brer Rabbit. "I'll hop into that
bucket and have a nap."

But as soon as he stepped into the bucket, it started going down the well.

"Ho! ho!" gasped Brer Rabbit. "Where am I going?"

Down, down went the bucket; the well was dark and cold and when, at last, the bucket hit the water the rabbit, very frightened, wondered what to do next.

Brer Fox had been watching Brer Rabbit and, thinking he was up to a trick, he followed him into the wood.
He saw him jump into the bucket and disappear.

"That's a funny thing to do," he muttered. "I wonder if Brer Rabbit keeps all his money down there?"

He peeped into the well and saw Brer Rabbit sitting in the bucket in the water.

"What are you doing down there?" he called to him.

"Oh, I'm fishing," replied Brer Rabbit. "I thought some fish would be a nice surprise for dinner for us all."

"Are there many down there?" asked Brer Fox, peering into the well.

"Oh, yes! Dozens and dozens of them!" answered Brer Rabbit. "Come and help me and we'll soon have enough for everyone."

"How can I get down?" the fox asked him.

"Just get into the other bucket," said Brer Rabbit, "that will bring you down."

Brer Rabbit seemed to be having a very good time and, as Brer Fox was fond of fish, he decided to join him.

Although he was rather big for the bucket, he managed to creep into it.

But, of course, he was much heavier than the little rabbit and, as his bucket went down, Brer Rabbit's bucket came up.

"Catch a nice bucketful of fish, Brer Fox!" cried Brer Rabbit as the buckets passed each other. "It's nice and cool down there!"

It was a long time before someone helped Brer Fox out of the well and, by that time, Brer Rabbit had run home.

BRER TERRAPIN SHOWS HIS STRENGTH

One day when the animals were feeling quite friendly towards each other, they started talking about the wonderful things they could do.

"I can run the fastest," boasted Brer Rabbit.

"And I am the sharpest," said Brer Fox.

"But I am certainly the strongest," said great big Brer Bear. He certainly looked the strongest, although he didn't move as quickly as some of the others.

Brer Terrapin thought for a little while. He wasn't very big, but he was quite cunning and he tried to think of a way to show off.

At last he said, "I think I can show you all that I am stronger even than Brer Bear!"

This made the other animals laugh.

"How ridiculous!" declared Brer Bear and Brer Fox.

But Brer Rabbit felt sure that Brer Terrapin was going to play a trick.

"Bring a strong rope and we'll go to the river," answered Brer Terrapin. "Then, see if Brer Bear can pull me out!"

So off they went.

When they reached the river, Brer Terrapin handed one end of the rope to Brer Bear.

"Take hold of that end," he said, "and walk away into the wood. I will hold this end and call out when you are to pull."

When they had gone out of sight,
Brer Terrapin dived into the river and
tied his end of the rope to the root of a
tree under the water.

Then he climbed out.

"Now pull!" he called to Brer Bear.

Brer Bear gave a little pull. He had hoped to pull the rope from Brer Terrapin very easily, but to his surprise it didn't move. So, he wrapped the rope around his paw and pulled harder, but still the rope didn't move.

"Pull harder!" called Brer Terrapin, jerking the rope.

Then Brer Bear put the rope over his shoulder and tugged and tugged, but he couldn't move it.

Next, all the animals tugged
together, but still Brer Terrapin sat
by the river holding the rope.
   At last he called . . .
   "Come back, I'm tired
of waiting."

As soon as he heard the others coming back, he dived into the river, untied the rope and sat on the river bank waiting for them.

"You tried hard," he said, "but you must agree that I'm just a bit stronger than you all!"

BRER RABBIT GOES SHOPPING

Brer Rabbit had such a good crop of corn that he decided to sell it and buy some of the things that Mrs. Rabbit was always asking for.

"We need tin plates and tin cups for the children," she told him, "and a new tin teapot."

So Brer Rabbit set off for market the next day.

"I've heard that Brer Rabbit is going to market to sell his corn," Brer Fox told his friends, Brer Wolf and Brer Bear. "Let's lie in wait for him and punish him for all the tricks he has played on us."

So they hid behind some trees by the roadside and waited.

Brer Rabbit soon caught sight
of them.

He tied all the tin plates and
cups around his neck and the tin teapot on his head. Then, with a
great cry, he dashed down the road.

"Here comes the tinker!" he yelled, clashing the plates
together. "I'm the iron man—look out for my iron teeth!"
Brer Fox, Brer Wolf and Brer Bear were terrified and ran off,
leaving Brer Rabbit to make his way safely home.

BRER RABBIT MEETS HIS MATCH

Brer Rabbit and Brer Buzzard decided to sew some seed and then to share the vegetable crop when it grew.

But when the time came for sharing out, there were no vegetables in the plot. As there was a very sly look on Brer Rabbit's face, Brer Buzzard felt sure Brer Rabbit had hidden them.

Brer Buzzard went away and thought very hard. The next day he called in to see Brer Rabbit.

"I've discovered a gold mine on the other side of the river," he said. "Come with me and we'll dig out the gold and share it."

"But how am I to cross the river?" asked Brer Rabbit.

"I'll carry you on my back," said Brer Buzzard, so Brer Rabbit scrambled up and off they went.

Instead of crossing the
water, Brer Buzzard perched
high up in a very tall tree in the
middle of the river.

Brer Rabbit didn't like this,
but Brer Buzzard kept laughing
and shaking until Brer Rabbit
was afraid he would fall off.

"Tell me where you have hidden all the vegetables we grew," demanded Brer Buzzard, "then we'll go back and divide them."

So Brer Rabbit had to agree and they flew back to his garden and shared the crop of vegetables he had hidden in his hut. But Brer Rabbit's knees shook with fright for a long time afterwards.

BRER RABBIT AND BRER LION

Most small animals were very frightened when a lion came to live near their homes.

"He says he must have three good meals a day," said Brer Fox, shivering to the tip of his tail.

"I'm not frightened," declared Brer Rabbit. "I'll finish off Brer Lion."

He went to the pond, wet his fur and rolled in the mud until he looked a miserable object.

Next, he crawled up to Brer Lion's den.

"I'm your three meals for today," he told him. "The other lion wants all the sheep and bullocks."

"Does he indeed?" roared Brer Lion. "Just lead me to him and we'll fight it out!"

So Brer Rabbit took him to the well near by and peeping in he cried . . .

"He's very fierce and angry! Don't go near him!"

When Brer Lion rushed to the well and looked in the water, he saw his own angry face and thought it was another lion.

"I'll fight you!" he cried. "We'll soon see who has the better meals!"

He dived in and was drowned and that was the end of Brer Lion.

"That's the way to deal with lions!" said Brer Rabbit.

BRER FOX AND MRS GOOSE

Mrs Goose was down by the water doing her washing one day when Brer Fox passed along on the other side of the river.

"Ha, ha!" he muttered. "That nice fat goose would make me a very tasty supper. I'll creep into her house tonight when she is asleep and catch her."

He didn't know that Brer Rabbit was listening to his plan but, as soon as the fox was out of sight, Brer Rabbit hopped over the stepping-stones to warn Mrs Goose.

"What shall I do?" wailed Mrs Goose in a great flutter. "I can't escape from that dreadful Brer Fox if he breaks into my house," and she cried and cried and made her washing wetter and wetter.

"Just listen to me," said Brer Rabbit, who was always ready to play tricks on Brer Fox, "make a bundle of your washing and put it in your bed, then fly up to the rafters and roost there for the night. I'll have a chat with Brer Dog, he will help you."

So that night, Mrs Goose did as Brer Rabbit had advised.

She made a big bundle of her washing and put it in her bed in a dark corner, then she flew up to the rafters and waited rather nervously to see what would happen.

Sure enough, at midnight, the door opened softly and Brer Fox crept in.

The room was so dark that it was easy to mistake the bundle of washing for a fine fat goose and Brer Fox, licking his lips, grabbed it and rushed out.

But Brer Dog was waiting
for him, and if the fox hadn't
dropped the bundle and run
for his life, he would certainly
have been caught.

The next morning the
story went around that
Brer Fox had tried to steal
Mrs Goose's washing!

All the animals
laughed and laughed to
think that the fine and
cunning Brer Fox had
wanted to steal anything
so silly as Mrs Goose's
washing!

THE MOON IN THE POND

One evening when all the animals were feeling friendly, they decided to go fishing together.

But when they reached the pond, Brer Rabbit looked very worried.

"Look!" he cried. "The moon has fallen into the water; we shan't catch any fish here until we have scooped it out."

So Brer Rabbit ran home to fetch a strong net.

"It seems to me," whispered Brer Fox, "that the moon is made of gold; I'm sure Brer Rabbit will try to keep it for himself so we mustn't let him get hold of it."

When Brer Rabbit came back with the net, Brer Fox took it from him.

"Let Brer Wolf and Brer Bear help me," he said, "you are too small to wade into the pond and pull that heavy moon from the water."

This was just what Brer Rabbit had planned so, while the big animals waded into the water, Brer Rabbit and his friend, Brer Tortoise, crept to the other side of the pond and started fishing.

Brer Fox, Brer Wolf and Brer
Bear waded deeper and deeper
into the water and tried to drag
the net around the moon but, of
course, as it was only the reflection
of the moon, they couldn't catch it.

Then Brer Fox slipped and Brer
Bear, stumbling over him,
clutched Brer Wolf and
they fell into the pond
with a mighty splash!

When they had struggled back to the bank they saw Brer Rabbit and Brer Tortoise hurrying away with a basket of fine fish.

"Tricked again!" they growled.

BRER RABBIT
AND THE HONEYPOT

Brer Rabbit was peeping through the grass one day when he saw Brer Bear walking down the road.

"I'll have a look inside Brer Bear's house," said the little rabbit, "there might be something nice to eat there."

He hopped along, and finding the door open, crept inside Brer Bear's house.

"Only bread and cheese on the table," grumbled Brer Rabbit. "I don't want that. I wonder what he keeps in the cupboard? Perhaps some lettuces or carrots or maybe a bag of oats."

Standing on a stool, Brer Rabbit opened the cupboard door.

"Nothing but cups and plates," muttered the rabbit, "except for that jar on the top shelf," and he stretched up a paw to reach it.

"O—oh!" over went the jar and out poured a stream of honey!

Poor Brer Rabbit was covered with sticky honey from head to foot, and although he licked and licked, it still stuck to him.

"Deary me!" he cried. "I like honey but not all over me! If I go out the bees will come after me and perhaps sting me if they think I've stolen their honey, and if I stay here Brer Bear will catch me."

At last he decided to run into the wood and roll in the leaves to rub off the honey.

This wasn't a very good idea for the leaves stuck to the honey and made Brer Rabbit look a terrifying person.

But when he saw that the other animals were frightened of him, he thought he might be able to scare his old enemy, Brer Fox, so he walked along waving his arms and making the leaves give a peculiar 'swishy' noise.

When Brer Bear saw him, he gave a howl and ran for his life and didn't stop until he was safely home.

The next animals Brer Rabbit met were Brer Fox and Brer Wolf.

They were busily making a plan to catch Brer Rabbit and didn't see him until he jumped onto a hillock in front of them.

"Gr—gr, I'm the Bogy Man!" shouted Brer Rabbit. "I eat bad wolves and foxes—I'll catch you both!"

"Help!" howled Brer Wolf.
"Help!" barked Brer Fox, as Brer Rabbit shook his leaf—covered paws in the air—and off they ran!

It took Brer Rabbit a long time to clean off the honey but how he laughed! And every time he saw Brer Fox he shouted—
"Mind the Bogy Man doesn't get you!"

BRER WOLF BREAKS THE LAW

As Brer Rabbit was walking along one day, he was thinking as usual of what tricks he could play on Brer Fox and Brer Wolf, but this time, he was nearly caught himself.

"Help! help!" came a voice from nearby and Brer Rabbit saw that Brer Wolf had been trapped under a great boulder.

"Please help me!" cried the wolf. "Give the boulder a push and set me free."

So Brer Rabbit, feeling rather sorry for the wolf although he didn't really like him, gave the boulder a mighty heave and out crawled Brer Wolf.

But instead of thanking Brer Rabbit, Brer Wolf seized him by the ears and declared he would have rabbit pie for dinner that night.

"That's a fine way to say thank you," squeaked Brer Rabbit, "I'll never do you a good turn again as long as I live!"

"You certainly won't!" laughed Brer Wolf.

Then Brer Rabbit thought quickly.

"Of course, you know, Brer Wolf that it's breaking the law to kill anyone who rescues you?" he said.

"No, I didn't know that," answered Brer Wolf, doubtfully.

"Well," said Brer Rabbit, "we must ask Brer Tortoise, he's the expert on these matters. There'll be trouble for you if you are proved wrong."

So Brer Wolf agreed to go to Brer Tortoise's house.

Brer Tortoise looked very wise when they asked for his opinion but, luckily, he was a friend of Brer Rabbit and wanted to help him.

"This is a very difficult case," he said at last when both animals had explained what had happened, "but we must be certain that the law isn't broken. Before I can decide, I must see the scene where this took place."

So off went the three animals.

Brer Tortoise poked the boulder and walked around it.

"There is only one way to decide," he said to Brer
Wolf, "I must see just how you were trapped."

So Brer Wolf crawled under the boulder and the tortoise
and the rabbit rolled it over him. Then Brer Tortoise said,

"Brer Rabbit, you were wrong. If you found Brer Wolf under
that boulder he was minding his own business and you should
have minded yours."

And Brer Tortoise and Brer Rabbit walked off and left Brer
Wolf to be rescued by someone else.

THE GREAT RACE

Brer Rabbit was very good at playing tricks on the other animals but sometimes they were too clever for him.

Brer Terrapin was walking slowly along the road one day when he met Brer Rabbit.

"Hello slow-coach!" laughed Brer Rabbit. "You look as though you're in a hurry!"

Brer Terrapin felt annoyed.

"I may be slow on land," he replied, "but I'm a good swimmer."

Brer Rabbit knew that although Brer Terrapin could swim, he was no quicker in the water than he was on the land.

"We'll have a race," said Brer Rabbit.
"I'll go by land and you can swim
in the river."
Brer Terrapin agreed to this,
so all the animals helped
them to measure
five miles along
the river path,
marking each mile
with a post.

Early next morning, Brer Terrapin put his wife and each of his four children at a post, then hid himself at the winning post.

All the terrapins looked the same, so when Mrs Terrapin dived into the water at the words

"Ready? Go!"
Brer Rabbit thought that she was Brer Terrapin.

He was surprised to see a terrapin swimming away from each mile post as he reached it.
"I didn't think Brer Terrapin could swim so fast!" he panted.

When he reached the winning post, he was amazed to find Brer Terrapin already there. "I'm tired of waiting for you," laughed the terrapin, "did you lose your way?"

Brer Rabbit simply couldn't understand what had happened.

How had Brer Terrapin arrived first at the winning post when he was such a slow coach?

But he was careful not to laugh at the terrapin next time he met him crawling along.

BRER FOX GOES HUNTING

Brer Fox went hunting one day and came back in the evening with a heavy bag over his shoulder. He didn't know that Brer Rabbit was watching him from the bushes.

"There must be something good in that bag," said Brer Rabbit to himself. "Perhaps I can trick Brer Fox into giving some of it to me; I would like a tasty morsel for my supper."

He ran on ahead of Brer Fox, pulled off his clothes and lay down in the middle of the road, pretending to be dead.

Along came Brer Fox and turned over the rabbit with his stick.

"Here's a fine fat rabbit," he declared, "and he seems to be dead. A pity I can't take him but I've as much as I can carry already," and off he went.

As soon as Brer Fox was out of sight, Brer Rabbit jumped up and, running through the woods, he lay down again in the road where he knew Brer Fox would find him.

"Well, this is a surprise," said Brer Fox, looking at the rabbit. "Another dead rabbit just waiting to be picked up. I think I'll leave my bag here and go back and collect the other one. It seems silly not to have them both. I'll bring another bag to put them in."

Off went Brer Fox thinking of the fine feast he would have; a bagful of birds and animals, and two fat rabbits as well.

"Just as I planned," laughed Brer Rabbit jumping up and putting on his clothes as soon as Brer Fox had disappeared down the road.

He snatched up the bag and trotted home with it.

"Tricked again!" growled Brer Fox when he discovered that the two dead rabbits had vanished as well as his bag and he had to go home without any supper.

HOW BRER RABBIT LOST HIS TAIL

Many years ago, Brer Rabbit had a long bushy tail rather like a squirrels; he was very proud of it and used to shake it as he walked.

One bright winter morning he met Brer Fox walking along carrying a string of fine fish.

"Those look good," said Brer Rabbit, "where did you catch them?"

"I caught them down in the river," answered Brer Fox. "There are plenty there."

"How did you catch them?" asked Brer Rabbit.

Brer Fox sat down on a log and tried to think for a moment how he could play a trick on Brer Rabbit.

"All you have to do," he said, "is to drop your tail into the water in the evening, and when you draw it up in the morning, it will be covered with fish."

"It sounds easy," thought Brer Rabbit.

So, that evening he put on his big warm coat and muffler, packed a basket of food and a hot drink, and set off to fish.

He sat on a big stone in the river and let his tail down into the water.

It was very, very cold and by morning poor Brer Rabbit felt quite frozen.

"I must be catching a fine lot of fish," he said to cheer himself up.

But when he tried to pull his tail out of the water, he found that it had frozen and as he got up, it snapped off! "Well, that was a trick," moaned poor Brer Rabbit looking at his stump of fluffy tail, "and no fish!"

And that is why rabbits now have little bob tails.

BRER RABBIT AND BRER BEAR

Brer Rabbit was very fond of green peas and lettuces, and when he found them growing in Brer Fox's garden, he crawled through the fence every day and had a good feast.

"I must set a trap," said Brer Fox, "someone is stealing my green peas and lettuces."

So he made a cunning trap by bending down a young tree just by the hole in the fence. He tied a rope to a high branch with a slip-knot at the end, then he fixed this on to a stick.

Next time Brer Rabbit
crept through the fence,
he knocked the stick away,
the rope caught him round
the legs and the tree sprang
back with Brer Rabbit
dangling in the air.
"Oh, dear!" he cried.
"I'm properly caught now!"

Just then, Brer Bear
came along.
"What are you doing
up there?" he asked.

"Making a pound a minute!" answered Brer Rabbit. "Brer Fox pays me to hang here and frighten the crows off his green peas and lettuces. But I'm very busy at present so, if you would like the job, you can take my place."

So Brer Bear helped Brer Rabbit down from the tree and fastened himself to a stronger part of the branch while Brer Rabbit ran away home with as much green stuff as he could carry.

"Ha! ha!" cried Brer Fox running from his house with a big stick. "So you're the thief who has been stealing my green peas and lettuces! Nicely caught Brer Bear!"

And poor Brer Bear got the punishment which should have been for Brer Rabbit.

"It's not always the biggest people who have the best brains," laughed Brer Rabbit as he enjoyed a meal of green peas and lettuces.